I Hate to Be the One to Tell You This

Zoë Walkington

smith|doorstop

the poetry business

Published 2023 by
Smith|Doorstop Books
The Poetry Business
Campo House,
54 Campo Lane,
Sheffield S1 2EG

ISBN 978-1-914914-41-6s
Typeset by Utter
Printed by People for Print

Smith|Doorstop Books are a member of Inpress:
www.inpressbooks.co.uk

Distributed by NBN International, 1 Deltic Avenue,
Rooksley, Milton Keynes MK13 8LD

The Poetry Business gratefully acknowledges the support of
Arts Council England.

Acknowledgements
'Hatton Garden' was published by *The North*; 'Shetland' was published by *Strix*

Contents

At Large

I can tell you about bad people.
How they will go through your cupboards.
One day you'll turn round from unloading the dryer,
and one will suddenly be there, in a balaclava,
only he won't call it a balaclava but a bally,
and you'll wish you'd listened when the dog, earlier,
barked and barked at what you thought was probably a fox.

Some of them will be apprehended in unusual places,
like on an EasyJet flight before it disembarks,
or at the top of a rickety iron ladder to an attic room,
or on a small boat coming in from a boating lake in York.
On arrest, some of them will be wearing a remembrance poppy
but mostly they are still at large, going about their business
Shopping at the big Tesco, grabbing a bag of Walkers Ready Salted.
Waiting in line at the petrol station.

Let me be your safeguarding concern

My first sight of Kent and Medway
was ricocheting out of the back
of a transit onto the A259
close to midnight.

The English police made the stop.
We heard their low murmuring voices,
van doors banging, from in the back.
I wasn't hanging about.

I had a cap on, from a place
I haven't been to. NYC
it said in red stitching.
The international signal for

not giving a shit.
I'd imagined London, but this
was all farms and no street lights.
Over the way, I heard dogs barking.

That night I slept on two
slightly damp bales of straw.
It wasn't raining, and I was safe
in the knowledge I didn't exist.

Whitby

You waited near the Harbour three long weeks that winter.
Finally, the ship sailed in, and from it lumbered a polar bear,
slow and grubby from the trip.

I watched him greet you, rubbing his huge head over your slim body,
your thin arms wriggling into his slack fur,
which, like in the stories, was torn,

and through the tear I saw, not golden threads, but denim,
and I knew then there was a man inside the bear.
A financial insolvent from an online dating site

who one day would discard his yellowed fur in the back-yard,
next to the old mattress. Now and then he would clout you with his paw,
but mostly it would be more ordinary than that.

Mostly it would be you, and him, and maybe a little bear,
sat at a Formica table eating porridge. You with one eye
on the harbour, looking at the ships.

I am not worth a farthing

Forgive me father
for I have sinned
and am not worth a farthing.
I am at a party with one boyfriend
let's call him the smaller one
when I get a WhatsApp from another
let's call him the bigger
and he says WHERE R U?
I'LL COME OVER
and father forgive me
but I think *Fuck me – no*
so I type back
that I am *AT CHOIR*
because it seemed very
innocent. Of all the places
I might be at that particular time
AT CHOIR seemed a good choice,
but for the small fact
that I can't sing
and am not in a choir
and never have been
and soon a WhatsApp comes back
AT CHOIR? R U ALED JONES?
And the panic rises
and I type back *JUST JOINED*
AM ALTO
and the bigger one replies
NOT ALED THEN? And a smiley face
and the little one says

Who are you texting?
and I say to him, and forgive
me for this father,
I say back to the little one
Oh piss off you insecure little prick.

Serial Liar

The last lie I told was in the eighties. It involved myself and two of the members of Fun Boy Three. Things turned litigious, so it was a calendar year before I would strike again, referring obliquely to the time I spent *inside* just enough for people to wonder if I could get them Ketamine, to take the edge off. So successful was that venture I let slip down at Claridge's that I could speak Russian. Made a point at parties of whispering into my own lapel. It didn't take long for the unmarked police cars to gather. Detectives, fat with latte, asleep under newspapers, kept me *under obvs*. I told the neighbours they weren't there for me but for *next door, organised crime, top brass*. I said it out of the corner of my mouth. I didn't make clear which side.

Hatton Garden

This is the last time we will wake up here,
the traffic already queuing on Great Portland Street.
Today is the last in a week of lies.
I pull on my suit, the tights
you washed the London smog out of.

I know, but you don't, what I'll say tonight.
You might phone home to Cork
in tears and disbelief,
or drink yourself blind with James
from the flat downstairs.

The small black hinged box will haunt
your drawer for weeks, maybe months,
and I know, but you don't,
that taking it back to Hatton Garden
would be best. They must get this all the time.

The Millstone Inn

You missed the last bus again. It's raining and it's 10.40pm. The pub lights are still on and your friends will all still be there but you can't go back in. Not now. The shell-shock hanging in the air like an inversion. While in time, some of you will forgive and forget, others will be cut off forever. Irrecoverable. Still, you meant every caustic word, watched each one burn into her pallid blue-veined skin. This is just a missed bus in the rain, no real reason to swallow your pride. Viewed through some lenses your exit could be seen as triumphant. The beads of diet coke still drying on the furniture. Besides which, they don't know that you are stood outside at the bus stop in the rain. They are sulking and glowering into their drinks picturing you on the top deck of the 272 to Sheffield, your feet dangling over the back of the chair in front, laughing like a Bonobo into your mobile phone.

"Some evidence for heightened sexual attraction under conditions of high anxiety."

In 1974 Dutton and Aron published a scientific study of romantic attraction on bridges

If a man meets a woman on a rickety bridge he is more likely to fall in love than if he meets her on a safe pavement, so psychologists would have it. Something to do with peril heightening the senses. Which, of course, is why I built my house on stilts next to the ricketiest I could find, one over a ravine, a raging torrent far below, rope for handrails and strung together planks for the feet, so in a high wind a person can progress only though a series of barely contained jack-knifes. What I have learned though, is that such bridges suffer from what retail graduates would call *low footfall*, and in the three long years I have lived here said footfall has been limited to just two men, both of whom teetered by when I was at the shops, buying rope with compromised tensile strength. Fortune might favour the brave, but the brave, it would seem, are either incredibly lazy or agoraphobic. Disheartened but undeterred, I am considering installing a toll booth to enforce interaction and charging fifty pence to all who wish to pass. As no one carries cash anymore the men will not only be in a high peril situation but will also be crestfallen which seems to me an almost perfect foundation for future romantic happiness.

Shetland

Arrival

We were warned of storms, but because we were eighteen we didn't expect them. We arrived in a waiting room that wore an outfit of cold white tiles. A one bar electric heater hung dangerously from the ceiling as if it might be there to kill flies, like in a butcher's shop. When you arrived my guts told me that if you offered me a Werther's Original I should refuse. It might be full of razor blades.

The house

No-one had used the bath for a month as it had been used to slaughter a pig in. There was a chest freezer with an exotic animal rolled into a ball inside. I think it was an armadillo. In your bedroom the cupboard had been modified to allow it to house chipmunks. Things looked promising.

The garden

There were twenty six dogs. I can only remember two of their names, Herman and Shithead. They were all housed in a shanty town of kennels crafted from old doors, bits of fridges and corrugated tin.

The work

We had to shovel shit using a bucket with no handle. We cut peat. We worked the kitchen garden where the carrots grew stunted because of Chernobyl.

The neighbours

Some were well intentioned, seemed concerned, but some just visited because we were eighteen, suntanned and pretty.

Your wife

She was meant to be there when we arrived but wasn't. She was in hospital. Her back twisted from too much lifting. That was the lie. She came home after two weeks, still bruised, around the time your home brew matured.

The wolf

The last time I saw you, you were drinking a pint, stood outside in the garden with your legs apart. That same night a wolf with a wounded paw came into the house, set itself up in the best chair in the lounge and started barking orders at everyone, snarling at the wife and frightening the mice in the kitchen. He slaked his thirst on the homebrew, slathered and panted after each pint, and ate pistachios, flicking the shells one after the other into the fire grate.

One night the wolf played Leonard Cohen records backwards at 4am, and I asked him, quite politely if he would turn the music down, so that we could sleep. The wolf stopped picking his teeth with the poker, turned to me and said *I shall play fuck with you if you touch my music* and no one ever looked deeper into my soul than the wolf did then. I went into the kitchen to reassure the mice, removed a knife from the knife block to keep under my pillow and once back inside my room we shunted the wardrobe to cover the door.

The dilemma

Inside the bedroom we could hear the wolf snarling and prowling in the hallway muttering that *someone was taking the piss*. A good thing because while I was the target of the wolf's chagrin, I knew the wife was safe, but it did demand that the wardrobe held fast.

How living with a wolf heightens the senses

We were hyper-vigilant, more awake than the lads from the boat club after a tab of speed, listening for signs that the wolf would turn on the

wife. He paced that hall for so long, and was so drunk he grew tired, and in the morning we found him asleep curled up on the hearth, his injured paw over his eyes, to stop the light from getting in.

Lies the dog has told me

That raw meat left on a work top overnight will crawl towards the dawn. That the rakish bloke with the cockerpoo bitch keeps looking at me. That to avoid litigation from vermin with an axe to grind, I should nail up his previous kills *as a warning* to other squirrels. That burglars entered the house, went through the bins, shredded the sofa, then left quietly. That it isn't true that he is 'catist', in fact some of his best friends are cats. That he can totally be trusted off-lead near cats. That he is allergic to my new boyfriend's dander.

Parklife

The dog has taken to offering unsolicited advice.
On leaving the house without him
he advises the local park would be best.
The one with the boating lake and the lawns.
Not to walk through briskly,
but rather to stand stock still
simultaneously channelling
barely contained aggression
and fear reactivity
while allowing men to approach
and sniff, slowly circling,
taking their time.
No sudden movements
he advises, no matter how close the nose.

I should judge these men
not on trivial matters –
postcode, profession, attire, –
but concentrate on the
carriage of their tail,
hackle deportment
and most of all their musk.
I express concerns, their own musk
may be covered by other musks
such as Paco Rabanne, or Issey Miyake?
The dog reassures me.
I will be able to tell
when a man has rolled in something.

Dog for sale

All sensible offers considered. Grey and white fur. Evil expression.

High prey drive. Generally of good character, with occasional lapses.

Prone to telling overblown lies about the activities of the neighbours.

Capable of a range of administrative tasks.

Familiar with most online banking systems.

Fond of *Compare The Meercat* and other price comparison sites.

Has his own online 'insta' influencer profile posting snaps of self in colour co-ordinated collar and lead sets posed louchely on variegated sofas.

Has passed Canine Good Citizen award (2017).

Obtained sponsorship deal from Pedigree Chum (2021) comprising a year's supply of Pedigree Chum (beef and rice flavour).

Does not eat Pedigree Chum (beef and rice flavour), only a raw diet consisting largely of squirrels, rabbits and, in a distressing case of mistaken identity, one chihuahua.

Tail un-docked as per kennel club guidance. Dew claws removed. No time wasters.

Imagine

bringing your mistress home to meet the family.
The low thump of the car doors.
The footsteps left behind her shoes
and your shoes, on the drive.

The shock on your wife's face.
Her mouth which for three years
you have only seen as a line
hangs open in a soft O.

Your kids not daring
to whisper to each other
What's a mistress?
Their legs and arms twining in perpetual motion.

Your mistress, you notice,
wears her handbag
over her forearm
as if she were carrying a basket of eggs.

She holds your wife's gaze
Smooths the crease in her pencil skirt.
In the silence she sniffs.
Looks the curtains up and down.

Yoga: A Users Guide

The regular practice of yoga over a five-year period will add 1cm to your height and remove £4,890 from your bank balance.

Every time you do a sun salutation the positive energy generated saves one aphid from a windscreen-based peril.

Yoga is a great way to meet other people who look like they would benefit from a good wash. Specifically, it is like nectar to hummus-eating men with man-buns.

When you lie on the ground in Savasana invisible roots push down through the earth and weave a warp and weft so in the event of an anti-gravity situation you won't fly off weightlessly and become separated from your yin and yan water bottle from Sweaty Betty (retail price £39.99).

When hungover in the yoga tent at festivals, it is best to avoid attempting to do 'bow pose', try it if you must, but believe me – you won't know whether to shit or go blind.

Yoga is the one thing you can claim to "practice" as a grown adult. It is unwise to make similar claims about driving a motorised vehicle or having sexual intercourse.

It is part of an ancient collective conscious passed down through the ages to think you are absolutely brilliant at yoga, until you practice in a room with a mirror.

The Last Psychic in Heptonstall

I am the last psychic in Heptonstall
my occupation now made derelict
by the advent of the internet.
People are catching on
that my portents regarding the length of journeys
they are about to take
are often significantly erroneous.
Somewhere near Halifax
a bloke named Barry
is keeping a spreadsheet of my failed predictions,
such as the fact that his grandmother
who, in 2018, I said was trying to get a message to him
from *the other side*, was actually buying liquorice,
in the pound shop at the time.
Also, he has noticed my health-related predictions
i.e. that a person will either get better
or get worse before getting better
can only turn out to be false
in clients who subsequently die.
Barry says, it's people like them,
the vulnerable dead ones, that he needs to speak for.

Happy Valley

I see the Kneževiés everywhere. They are the window cleaners casing the joint or they're lurking in Audis stopped in dead end car parks. The milkman is probably paying them menaces in double cream, or brown envelopes fat with cash - who knows. The florists too are being skimmed, the top quarter of each gladioli going to pay their dark debts.

On the high street, every-one knows but nobody dares mention, apart from Catherine, stout against the stitches of her bulky black uniform. Sensible shoes hefting her from one incident to another, all of them linked, but only she can see how. Patron saint of parting shots, and always slightly out of puff, on the in-breath drinking tea, saying *daft twats* on the out.

Walking past a canal boat my heart quickens. He's probably in there, a can of petrol and his dulcet Yorkshire tones. He's likely gaming or growing his amazing auburn hair for that hair- dresser with the clippers. The one who is still inside, working for tuna by the tin. A lifer I'll bet and he'll need to serve a long old stretch to crop another such head of hair.

Perhaps though, Tommy's gone straight, taken up Parkour, escaping the pavements like a baboon, he's probably up there now on top of Leeds Crown Court – laughing against the breeze or possibly crying if any countryside is in view. He loves a vista does Tommy.

I picture us together up Mam Tor, eating sandwiches. Me stealing side glances at him, as he threatens the sheep Yorkshirely, *Off yer fuck* he will scatter the brave ones, the ones that want in on our crisps *Off yer fuck*. He'll look up and smile at me as he chews. In the valley bottom, I will spot a van winding the country road. Gaining on us. Still gaining.

U-bend

My plumber swears his flexibility is such that he is able to fold himself
into a standard oven cavity, providing you remove all the shelves.

I have met men like him before, who on receipt of two sugars in their
tea are prone to overblown claims, like that they are Elvis or they can
undo a button using only their tongue.

I remove each metal shelf, one by one, never once breaking eye
contact, expecting him to crack under the pressure. Instead, he sets
down his tea and begins an elaborate routine of stretches and bends,
working his muscles slack, mixing in some high intensity drills like a
footballer.

I stand in my kitchen watching him do high kicks, groin stretches,
and at one point I swear, an old-school crab. I think of the bowerbirds
of South America as he dislocates each hip in preparation.

Ready? I enquire, one eyebrow cocked. He tells me he was *born ready*
and commences his contortions for real. Arse first, he posts himself in
backwards un-jointing first his left knee, then the right to fold them
yogically in front of himself.

His feet he rachets round like a faulty handbrake. The first arm
is an easy retraction, the second more challenging and I think of
commuters at Stockport station folding their Bromptons with a
satisfying clunk as he uses his last free hand to twist his head
into place.

Whilst it's hard for him to speak now he is able to manage a muffled
Ta-Daaar. To be fair, I AM impressed, but say nothing, shut the door.
Turn the dial to two hundred.

Decimal point

After the great decimal point error of 2021
the milk man was £3750 richer
and I the same poorer.
I pictured him whining down the dark street
in his milk-float
straight to Thomas Cook
to book his trip to Mexico
where he might buy a Poncho
drink the night away at the fully inclusive bar
and in the morning
lie in until seven.
Or perhaps the following day
I would open the door
to bottles of skimmed, semi, full fat
that fill the driveway
the neighbours gardens
the street, passing walkers
marooned by clinking bottles
as far as the eye can see
still beaded with cool.

Utility Breed

There's a dog at the door, and I hate to say this, but it's about the electric, and he says he wants our sausages, and he's got a warrant to take them, and he's slathering, and his tail is held high and stiff, and his clipboard has spots of blood on it, from the all others he's hounded. He's got a lanyard with a picture of himself, but much smaller, and in the picture he's grinning, and his fangs are glinting, and his fur is combed all perfect like he's just got back from the groomers. But that's not what he looks like now, stood on his hind legs, with one paw jammed in the door so I can't shut it. And he's vaping and he's blowing the smoke into our hallway, and it doesn't smell of vanilla but of beef and tripe, and he just keeps saying how *hungry* he is, and he's looking at me like I might be a snack, and his hackles are rising, and if I didn't know better I might say he looked like a dangerous breed, the banned sort, that shouldn't be working as a bailiff or for E-ON, and he can read my thoughts, because he is up in my grill now, and he is barking at me *I am not one of the banned breeds, you low life scum. I am a working dog.*

Woburn Sands Hand Car Wash & Valeting

There are five of them
one tells me when to pull forward,
two squirt me with suds and get flannelling.
The four-by-four rocks as they go up
onto my wheel tops for the roof
their trousers pressed against
my windows on both sides.
They don't seem as excited as me
I have to stop myself shouting
YES. YES. YES.
They sluice me down.
Under instruction, I drive just
ten metres forward
then all five are on me
with the shammy leathers
all talking to each other
sucking up my water and dirt
as if it happens every day
to have men pressed up against
windows, making the car jiggle and bob.

Ducks

At first they're always under my feet,
peep-peeping and following as I move
from dishwasher to table and back.
They gulp down the grubs and earthworms
I catch, after heavy rain, cutlery fork in hand,
glasses on, standing on one leg like a heron, on the lawn.

Back inside, they circle my feet
peep as loud as tiny whistles
The two bravest peck at my socks with their bills.
I toss worm after worm, grub after grub,
and overnight each duckling's outline expands
as if traced over by a thick pen.

In a week they've doubled in size
and soon they outgrow the washing up bowl,
one always popping over the side.
I move the coffee table and inflate a paddling pool
between my sofas – filling it
with bucket after bucket from the cold tap.
The ducklings bob and splash their content.

Before long the harvest from the back garden
is not enough and I mine the rockery at the front.
The neighbours become inquisitive and I fret
the double glazing will betray me,
the peeps turning into braying quacks.

I become pale. Aldi seems a long way away
and besides, the grubs aren't so bad.

Catching myself in the mirror one day
I brush soil from the corners of my mouth.
My lips harden and crack.

When the paddling pool develops a tear
I put the plug in the sink
move the dishcloth to the granite island,
turn the tap on and wait.
Flooding the floor takes three hours.
Within a day the electrics blow.
We leak surprisingly little, top up just once a day.

Nights are the best. We roost on the granite island
caked with poo. Our breath one rhythm, our feathers puffed.
The two drakes lie awake longer than the rest,
perched on the knife block, blinking into the night.